MACHINES ON THE MOVE

MAIL TRUCKS

by Natalie Deniston

TABLE OF CONTENTS

Tadpole Books, an imprint of Jump! Library by FlutterBee

tadpole books

WORDS TO KNOW

bins

drives

mail

mailbox

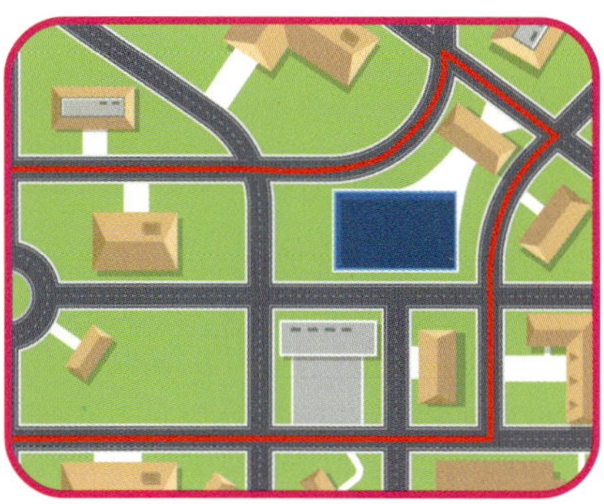

path

post office

MAIL TRUCKS

This is a post office.

Inbound / Outbound Staging Area
Dock Door 82
Dock Door 81
UNITED STATES POSTAL SERVICE
DO NOT CUT
ESIGNED FOR MULTIPLE USE
PROPERTY OF USPS
RECYCLE
UNITED STATES POSTAL SERVICE
DO NOT CUT
DESIGNED FOR MULTIPLE USE
PROPERTY OF USPS
RECYCLE
PRIORITY MAIL

H-3
220-223
ED STATES
POSTAL SERVICE
DO NOT CUT
DESIGNED FOR MULTIPLE USE
PROPERTY OF USPS
RECYCLE
UNITED STATES
POSTAL SERVIC
DO NOT CUT
DESIGNED FOR MULTIPLE U
PROPERTY OF USPS
RECYCLE
PRIORITY
MAIL
K3 B42

Mail is here.

Mail goes in bins.

It goes in a truck.

The truck drives.

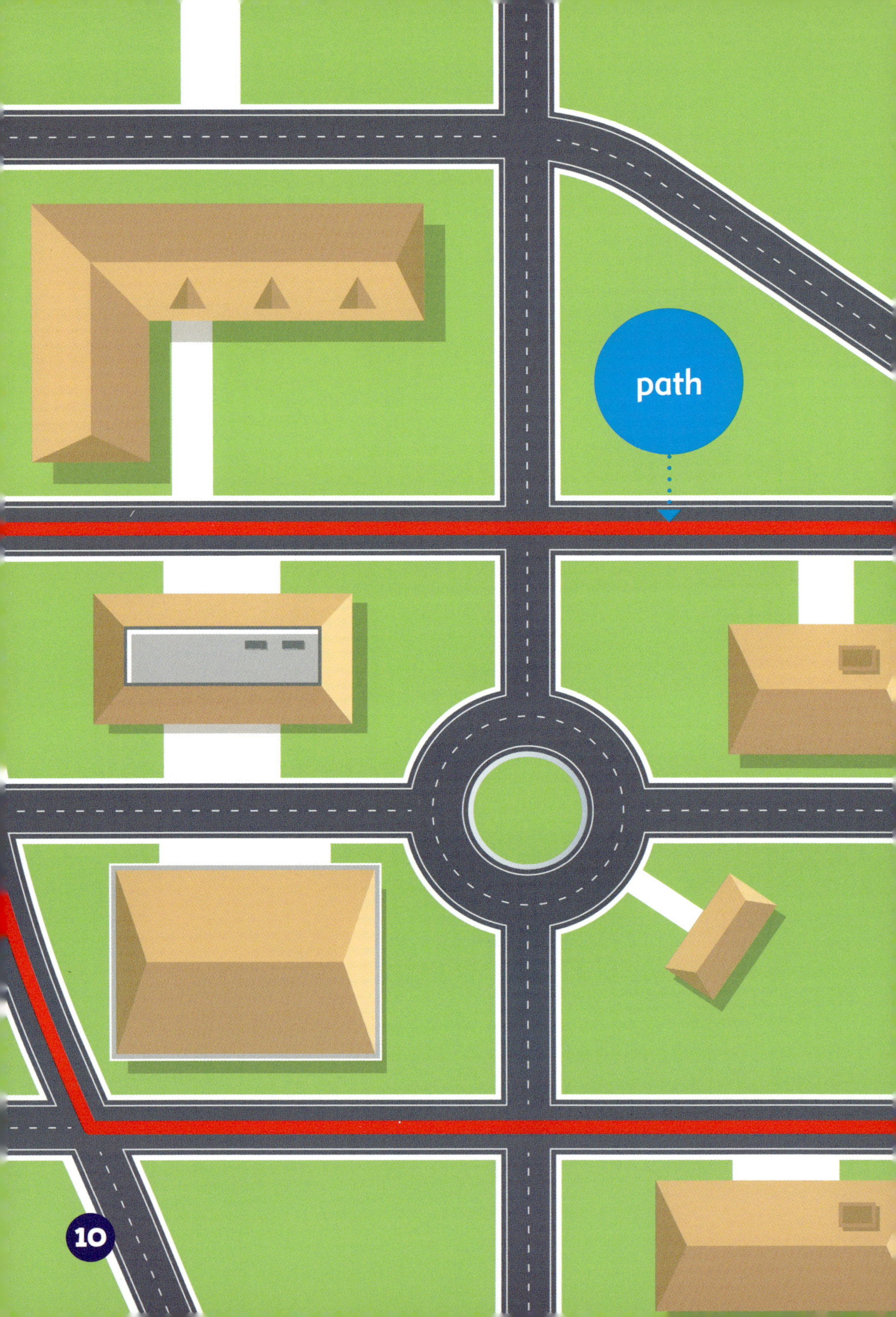
path

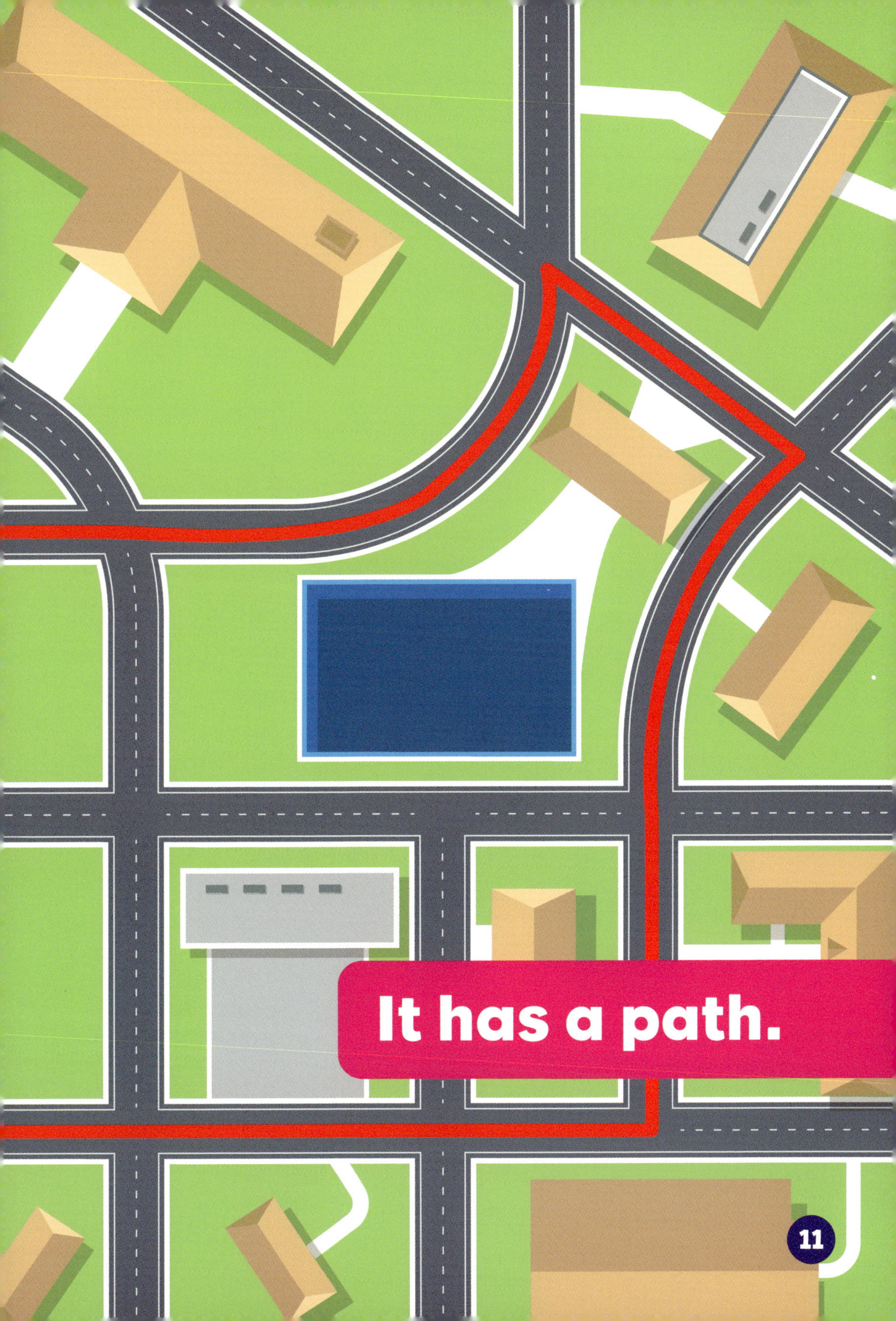

It has a path.

It stops.

Mail goes in a mailbox.

UNITED STATES
POSTAL SERVICE

Thank you!

LET'S REVIEW!

Mail trucks bring us mail. What colors are a mail truck?

INDEX